Around the Neighborhood

HOUGHTON MIFFLIN HARCOURT
School Publishers

Contents

TEKS **1.3A** decode words in context and in isolation; **1.3C(i)** decode using closed syllables; **1.3H** identify/read high-frequency words

Phonics

Words with Short <u>a</u> Read each sentence. Then point to and read words with the short <u>a</u> sound. Tell which picture the sentence is about.

Dan sat.

I am a cat.

Dan and Nan

by Evan MacDonald
illustrated by Lorinda Bryan Cauley

I am Dan Cat.

Dan Cat sat.

I am Nan Cat.

Nan Cat sat.

Dan sat. Nan sat.

Dan and Nan can play.

Letters

Names A name begins with a capital letter. Read the names. Say the letters in each name.

Dan   **Nan**

Write your name. Say each letter. Which letter is a capital letter? Name the lower-case letters.

9

TEKS 1.3A decode words in isolation; **1.3B** apply letter-sound knowledge to create words; **1.3C(i)** decode using closed syllables

Phonics

Words with Short <u>a</u> Read these words.

| c | a | t | | s | a | t |

Read the words on the path.

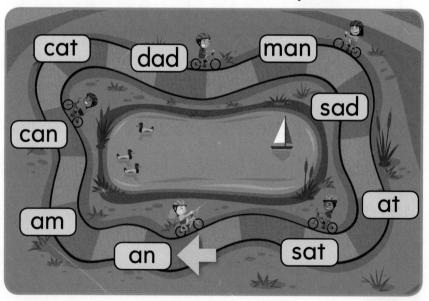

Nat Cat

by Uta Tibi
illustrated by Noah Jones

Nat Cat sat.

Nan sat.

Tad sat.

Nan can play with Tad.

Nat! Nat! Nat Cat!

Nan, Tad, and Nat can play.

TEKS **1.3H** identify/read high-frequency words; **1.3I** monitor decoding accuracy; **1.5** read aloud with fluency/comprehension **ELPS** **4A** learn English sound-letter relationships/decode

Fluency

Read Together

Words to Know You have to remember some words. Read these words.

| play | with | and |

Letter-Sounds Letter-sounds can help you read other words. Read these names.

| Nan | Tad | Nat |

Read Aloud Work with a partner. Take turns reading aloud "Nat Cat." Help each other read words correctly.

Phonics

Words with Short <u>a</u> Read the sentences. Then point to and read words with the short <u>a</u> sound. Name the girl and her pet in the pictures.

Fan can nap.

Pam can play.

Fan, Fan, Fan

by Graham Neu

Pat sat. Pat can be a fan.
Fan, fan, fan, fan.

Dan sat. Dan can be a fan.
Fan, fan, fan, fan.

Nan sat. Nan can be a fan.
Fan, fan, fan, fan.

Sam sat. Sam can be a fan.
Fan, fan! Fan, fan!

Pam sat. Pam can be a fan.
Fan, fan! Fan, fan!

23

Can you be a fan?
Fan! Fan! Fan! Fan!

TEKS 1.17A generate ideas for writing; 1.17E publish/share writing   ELPS 5B write using new basic/content-based vocabulary

Writing

Plan   Are you a fan? What activity do you love to watch?

Write   Draw a picture. Write about the picture. You can use these sentences: **I like** _____.
I am a big fan. Share your work with classmates.

25

TEKS **1.3A** decode words in context and in isolation; **1.3C(i)** decode using closed syllables; **1.3H** identify/read high-frequency words

Phonics

Words with Short i Read each riddle. Find the picture that answers it. Point to and read the short i words.

It has a fin. What is it?

Sid can hit it. What is it?

A cat can rip it. What is it?

Can It Fit?

by Chandra Majors
illustrated by Elizabeth Allen

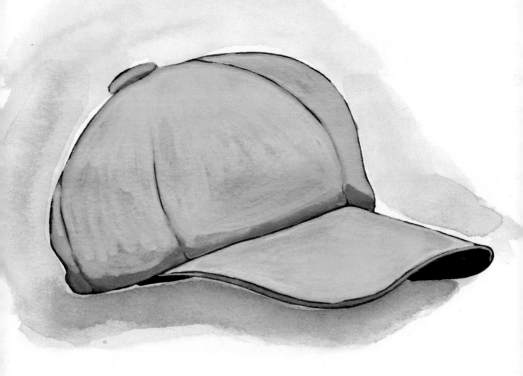

It is a tan cap.
What can fit in it?

27

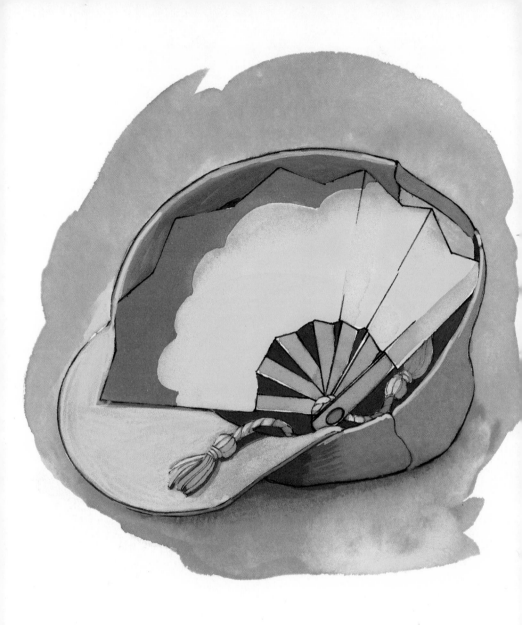

A fan can fit in it.
Is it for a fan?

A tin pan is in it.
Is it for a tin pan?

A map can fit in it.
Is it for a map?

Ram Cat can sit in it.
Is it for Ram Cat?

Look at Sam!
It is his cap
Ram is his cat.

Fluency

Read Together

Punctuation Marks Read these sentences. Each sentence should sound different. Use the end marks to help you.

Can it fit?
It can fit.
It can fit!

Read Aloud Work with a partner. Use end marks to help you read aloud "Can It Fit?"

Phonics

Words with Short i Read the words on each ladder. Tell which words have the short i sound.

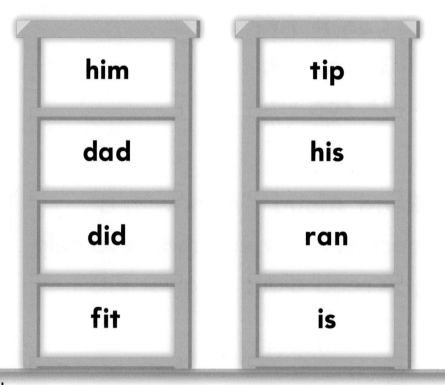

him	tip
dad	his
did	ran
fit	is

I Ran

by Chris Gericho

Pam ran.

Tif did, too.

Dad is with Pat.
Dad ran. Pat ran.

Sid ran, ran, ran.

Tip is with him.

Look at Tim.

Tim ran. Nan did, too.

Dan ran, ran, ran!
Tam ran. Cam did, too.

I ran, ran, ran!
Did you?

TEKS 1.28 share information/ideas by speaking clearly ELPS 3E share information in cooperative learning interactions

Speaking

Read Together

Share Think about these questions:

- When do you run?
- Do you like to run?

Tell a partner about running. Use these tips.

Speaking Tips

- Speak clearly and loudly enough to be heard.
- Do not speak too fast or too slowly.

Phonics

Words with Short i Read the clues. Tell which pet each clue is about. Point to and read the short i words.

It is big and can sit.

It is little and can dig.

Pam

by Tony Manero
illustrated by Jeff Shelly

Tip has a bat.
It is for Pam.

Did Pam bat?
Pam sat!

Rip has a cap.

It is for Pam.

Pam has a cap!
Pam has a bat, too.

Pam is at bat.
Can Pam hit it?

Bam! Pam did it!
It is a big, big hit!

TEKS **1.3A(i)** decode words with consonants; **1.1B** identify upper- and lower-case letters; **1.21B(iii)** capitalize names of people; **ELPS** **4A** learn English sound-letter relationships/decode

Letters

Read Together

Identify Names

| Tip | cap | Pam | bat | Rip |

1. Point to and read three names. What kind of letter do they begin with?
2. Point to and read the word that ends with **t**. Is it a name? How do you know?
3. Read each word. Which words are names and which are not? How do you know?

Phonics

Words with Short o Read each word. Then use the words in sentences. Try to use two or more words in one sentence.

mop	top	pot
box	log	hop

Lil and Max

by Alexis Davis
illustrated by Akemi Gutierrez

Lil got a big, big mop.
Can Lil and Max sit on top?

Can they do it? No!

Max got a big, big pot.
Can Lil and Max hop on it?

Hip, hop. Hip, hop, hop.
Lil and Max hop in it!

Lil and Max find a cot.
It is a big, big, BIG cot!

Lil can sit on top!
Max can sit on top, too!

TEKS **1.3A(ii)** decode words with vowels; **1.3D** decode words with common spelling patterns; **1.6D** categorize words **ELPS 4A** learn English sound-letter relationships/decode

Spelling Patterns

Read Together

Sort Words Read these words. How are they alike?

| mop | fox | got | pot | hop | box |

Copy this chart. Write two words in each column. Read the words again. How are the words in each column alike?

_op	_ot	_ox

Phonics

Words with Short o Read each question and answer it. Then point to and read words with the short o sound.

Can the dog fit in the box?

Can the dog sit on the box?

Can the dog fix the box?

Did Dix Dog Do It?

by Oliver Berry
illustrated by Mike Gordon

Dad Dog is sad.
Dad has to fix it.
Did Dix Dog do it?

Sal Dog is sad.

Did Dix Dog do it?

Mom Dog is sad.

It is not funny!

Did Dix Dog do it?

Lon Dog is sad.
Did Dix Dog do it?

Doc Dog is sad.
Did Dix Dog do it?

No! Max Cat did it!

Book Information

Read Together

Book Parts The arrows point to the title, the name of the author, and the name of the illustrator.

title ——
author ——
illustrator ——

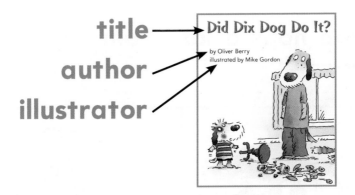

Did Dix Dog Do It?

by Oliver Berry
illustrated by Mike Gordon

What do you like about the author's words? What do you like about the illustrator's art?

Phonics

Words that End with -s Read each sentence pair. Which is Rob? Which is Pam?

Rob can hop. Pam can dig.

Rob hops a lot. Pam digs a lot.

Is It Funny?

by Laurence Christopher
illustrated by Liz Callen

Pat can tap.

Pat taps, taps, taps.

Hal is not sad.
Hal sits in his box.

Ron Dog is hot.
Pat fans the hot dog.

Hal can sing.
Hal sings a rap.

Pat has a big pot.

Pat can mix a lot.

Hal has a pad.
What is on it?
It is funny!

TEKS **1.3A(ii)** decode words with vowels; **1.6A** identify nouns/verbs **ELPS 1C** use strategic learning techniques to acquire vocabulary; **4A** learn English sound-letter relationships/decode

Vocabulary

Action Words

| tap | sit | fan | hop | mix |

Act It Out Work with a partner. Read the words. Then write each word on a card. Place the cards face-down. Pick a card and act out the word. See if your partner can guess the word. Then have your partner act out a word and you try to guess the action.

Phonics

Words with Short <u>e</u> Read these words.

p e t   l e t

Read the words on the path. Tell which words have the short <u>e</u> sound.

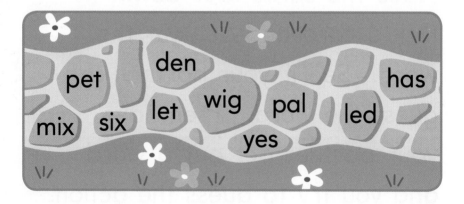

74

Pals

by Aiden Brandt

Len and his pals can hop!
Len led all his pals.

Lin has a pet dog.
Wags is a good pal!

Wes let his pals in.

His pals can play in his den.

Can Mom be a pal?
Yes! Mom and Ben get logs.

Six pals ran six laps.
Who led the pals? Mel did!

Ted sat on a big log.
Ted sat with his pals.

TEKS 1.1A recognize that print represents speech **ELPS** 5A use English sound-letter relationships to write

Words in Print

Read Together

Speech Print can show what people say. Look at the photo. In the story, Len and his pals hop. Read what Len is saying.

My pals and I can all hop.

Draw and Write Draw a picture of yourself talking to a friend. Write what you say.

Phonics

Words with Short e Read the words. Find three short e words in a row. Read those words again.

sat	wig	pet
bed	yes	ten
win	get	his

Ned

by David McCoy
illustrated by Neena Chawla

Here is Ned.
Who is he?

83

Ned is not Ned Pig.
Ned is not Ned Ox.
Ned is Ned Hog.

Is Ned Hog big? Yes!
Does Ned have ten wigs? No!
Ned Hog has ten hats!

Ned has a cap, too.

Ned Hog is at bat.

Can he get a big hit? Yes!

Ned Hog is hot.
It is not hot in here.
Ned can nap in his bed.

Who is Ned Hog?

Ned is top hog!

Ned wins, wins, wins!

TEKS 1.1B identify upper- and lower-case letters; **1.21B(i)** capitalize beginning of sentences; **1.21B(iii)** capitalize names of people

Letters

Identify Letters Names begin with a capital letter. Sentences begin with a capital letter, too. Here is a sentence about Ned Hog:

Can Ned Hog get a big hit?

Which words begin with capital letters? Which are names? What word begins the sentence? Why does the word *hit* begin with a lower-case letter?

TEKS **1.3A** decode words in context and in isolation; **1.3C(i)** decode using closed syllables; **1.3H** identify/read high-frequency words

Phonics

Words with Short <u>e</u> Read each sentence. Point to and reread the short <u>e</u> words. Then tell which picture matches each sentence.

Vic gets his jet.
Ken has a pen.

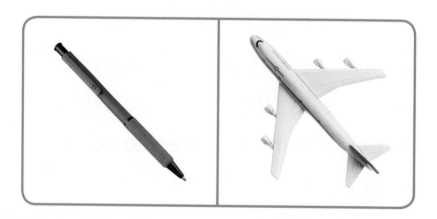

My Pets

by Alice Ling

illustrated by Meryl Treatner

Big Vic is my pet dog.

Kit is my pet cat.

Kit can get six red jets.
Get the jets, Kit!

Big Vic can get ten tin men.
Here, Big Vic. Get set. Go!

Kit and Big Vic nap in the den.
Kit and Big Vic nap with me.

Big Vic and Kit get fed.
Sit, Big Vic, sit!

Kit fits in the cat bed.
Big Vic does not fit in it.
Big Vic does not fit in my bed!

TEKS **1.27A** listen attentively/ask relevant questions; **1.29** follow discussion rules **ELPS 2I** demonstrate listening comprehension of spoken English

Listening

Listen for information   Join a small group. Take turns talking about pets you have or would like to have. Use the tips.

Listening Tips

- Look at the person who is talking.
- Listen carefully to hear the information.
- Raise your hand to ask a question or to speak.

Phonics

Words with Short <u>u</u> Read and answer each question. Then point to and read the short <u>u</u> words.

Is the pup up on a bed?   yes no

Is the pup on a bus?   yes no

Is the pup on a rug?   yes no

Fun in the Sun

by Norman Swaderski
illustrated by Stephen Lewis

Jen Pig is hot.
Can Jen hop in? No!

Ed Hog is hot.

Can Ed hop in? Yes!

Ed has fun, fun, fun!

Ed pulls his friend.
Tug, tug. Hold on, Jen.

Can Jen hop in? Yes!
Jen has fun, fun, fun!

Ed Hog hops up, up, up!
Jen Pig hops up, up, up!

Ed has fun in the sun.
Jen has fun in the sun, too!

Decoding

Read Together

Read Carefully Read this story.

> The sun is up. Jen is hot. Can Ed get Jen in the mud? Yes! Ed and Jen can play in the mud!

Think Do you think you read every word correctly? How do you know? If a word is hard to read, how can you figure it out? Reread the story.

TEKS 1.3A decode words in isolation; **1.3C(i)** decode using closed syllables

Phonics

Words with Short <u>u</u> Read each word. Then use the words in sentences. Use two or more words in one sentence.

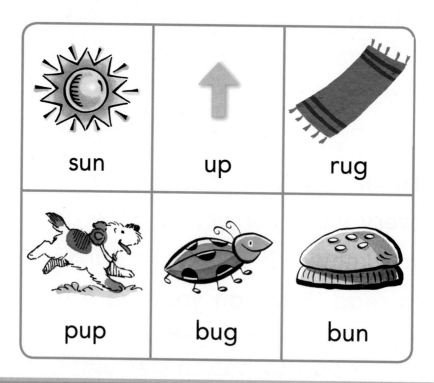

sun	up	rug
pup	bug	bun

Yams! Yum!

by Rona Blanca
illustrated by Gina Freschet

Yak is in bed,
but he has to get up.

Yak has to get yams.
What can Yak do?

Can Yak get big, fat yams?
Yes! He can get lots and lots.

Yak can set his yams in a bag.
His red bag can hold lots!

Yak can fit ten yams in his bag.
His bag is full. Yams! Yum!

Yak has his yams.
He has lots and lots.
Yams! Yum, yum, yum!

TEKS 1.1A recognize that print represents speech; **1.19A** write brief compositions **ELPS** 5A use English sound-letter relationships to write

Words in Print

Read Together

Speech Remember that print can show what people say. Look at the picture. Read what Yak says about yams.

I can fit ten big, fat yams in my red bag.

Draw and Write Draw yourself talking to a family member about your favorite food. Write what you say.

Phonics

Words with Short <u>u</u> Read all the words. Then find three short <u>u</u> words in a row. Read those words again.

run	zip	jug
tug	yes	mud
yum	quit	van

Bud

by David McCoy
illustrated by Jeffrey Ebbeler

Bud is a pug. Bud is a pup.
Bud can fit in a big cup!

Bud digs in the mud.
Quit it, Bud! Quit it!

Zip!   Bud hops in the tub.

Rub, rub!   Rub-a-dub-dub!

Bud has fun!

Bud sits with us.
We play. Bud naps.

Bud can help us.
Bud gets many hugs!

Bud can tug. Bud can run.
Bud has fun in the hot sun.
Good dog, Bud!

Words

High-Frequency Words With a partner, write each of these words on two cards:

> good   many   play   help   with

Word Game Lay the cards upside down on a table. Take turns choosing two cards. Read the words. If they match, keep them. If they don't, put them back. Who can make the most matches?

TEKS **1.3A** decode words in isolation; **1.3B** apply letter-sound knowledge to create words; **1.3C(i)** decode using closed syllables; **1.3D** decode words with common spelling patterns;

Phonics

Read to Review Use what you know about sounds and letters to read the words.

Short <u>a</u>

cat	hat	dad	sad
man	pan	bag	tags

Short <u>i</u>

big	dig	pig	pit
his	six	rip	sits

Short <u>o</u>

hot	dot	lot	box
fox	top	hops	jobs

1.3E read words with inflectional endings; **ELPS 2B** recognize elements of English sound system; **3A** practice sounds/pronunciation of English words

Short e̲

pet	set	get	pen
ten	beds	yes	legs

Short u̲

up	sun	fun	rug
tub	bus	bugs	cups

Build and Read Words   Put the letters together to read the words. Think of more words to add.

b at	b it	n et
m at	f it	l et
s at	k it	w et

123

Word Lists

Dan and Nan
page 2

Decodable Words
Target Skill: Short *a*
am, can, Cat, Dan, Nan, sat

Target Skills: Consonants *n, d*
can, Dan, Nan

High-Frequency Words
New
and, play

Previously Taught
I

Nat Cat
page 10

Decodable Words
Target Skill: Short *a*
can, Cat, Nan, Nat, sat, Tad

Target Skills: Consonants *n, d*
can, Dan, Nan, Tad

High-Frequency Words
New
and, play, with

Accompanies
"What Is a Pal?"

Fan, Fan, Fan

page 18

Decodable Words

Target Skill: Short *a*
can, Dan, fan, Nan, Pam, Pat, Sam, sat

Target Skills: Consonants *p, f*
fan, Pam, Pat

Target Skills: Consonants *n, d*
fan, can, Dan, Nan

High-Frequency Words

New
be, you

Previously Taught
a

125

Accompanies *"The Storm"*

Can It Fit?

page 26

Decodable Words
Target Skill: Short *i:*
fit, his, in, is, it, sit, tin

Target Skills: Consonants *r, h, /z/s*
has, his, is, Ram

Words with Previously Taught Skills
can, cap, Cat, fan, map, pan, Sam

High-Frequency Words
New
for, look, what

Previously Taught
a

I Ran

page 34

Decodable Words
Target Skill: Short *i*
did, him, is, Sid, Tif, Tim, Tip

Target Skills: Consonants *r, h, /z/s*
him, is, ran

Words with Previously Taught Skills
at, Cam, Dad, Dan, Nan, Pam, Pat, Tam

High-Frequency Words
New
look, too

Previously Taught
I, with, you

Pam

page 42

Decodable Words

Target Skill: Short *i*
big, did, hit, is, it, Rip, Tip

Target Skills: Consonants *b, g*
bam, bat, big

Target Skills: *r, h, /z/s*
has, hit, is, Rip

Words with Previously Taught Skills
at, can, cap, has, Pam, sat

High-Frequency Words

New
for, too

Previously Taught
a

Lil and Max

page 50

Decodable Words
Target Skill: Short *o*
cot, got, hop, mop, on, pot, top

Target Skills: Consonants *l, x*
Lil, Max

Words with Previously Taught Skills
big, can, hip, in, is, it, sit

High-Frequency Words
New
do, find, no, they

Previously Taught
a, and, too

Did Dix Dog Do It?

page 58

Decodable Words
Target Skill: Short *o*
Doc, Dog, Lon, Mom, not

Target Skills: Consonants *l, x*
Dix, fix, Lon, Max, Sal

Words with Previously Taught Skills
Cat, Dad, did, has, is, it, sad

High-Frequency Words
New
do, funny, no

Previously Taught
to

Is It Funny?

page 66

Decodable Words

Target Skill: Short *o*
box, Dog, dog, hot, lot, not, on, pot, Ron

Target Skill: Inflection -*s*
fans, raps, sits, taps

Target Skills: *l*, *x*
box, Hal, lot, mix

Words with Previously Taught Skills
big, can, has, his, in, is, it, pad, Pat, rap, sad, tap

High-Frequency Words

New
funny, sing

Previously Taught
a, and, the

129

Pals

page 74

Decodable Words
Target Skill: Short *e*
Ben, den, led, Len, let, Mel, pet, Ted, Wes, yes

Target Skills: Consonants *y, w*
Wags, Wes, yes

Words with Previously Taught Skills
big, can, did, dog, get, has, his, hop, in, is, laps, Lin, log, logs, Mom, pal, pals, ran, sat, six

High-Frequency Words
New
all, who

Previously Taught
a, and, be, good, play, the, with

Ned

page 82

Decodable Words
Target Skill: Short *e*
bed, get, Ned, ten, yes

Target Skills: Consonants *y, w*
win, wigs, yes

Words with Previously Taught Skills
at, bat, big, can, cap, has, hats, his, hit, Hog, hot, in, is, it, nap, not, Ox, Pig, top

High-Frequency Words
New
does, here, who

Previously Taught
a, have, he, no, too

My Pets

page 90

Decodable Words

Target Skill: Short *e*
bed, den, fed, get, jets, men, pet, pets, red, set, ten

Target Skills: Consonants *k, v, j*
jets, Kit, Vic

Words with Previously Taught Skills
Big, can, cat, dog, fit, fits, in, is, it, nap, not, sit, six, tin

High-Frequency Words

New
does, here, me, my

Previously Taught
and, go, the, with

Fun in the Sun
page 98

Decodable Words
Target Skill: Short u
fun, sun, tug, up

Words with Previously Taught Skills
can, Ed, has, his, Hog, hop, hops, hot,
in, is, Jen, on, Pig, yes

High-Frequency Words
New
friend, hold, pulls

Previously Taught
and, no, the, too

Yams! Yum!
page 106

Decodable Words
Target Skill: Short *u*
but, up, yum

Words with Previously Taught Skills
bag, bed, big, can, fat, fit, get, has, his,
in, is, lots, red, set, ten, Yak, yams, yes

High-Frequency Words
New
full, hold

Previously Taught
a, and, do, he, to, what

Bud

Decodable Words

Target Skill: Short *u*
Bud, cup, dub, fun, hugs, mud, pug, pup, rub, run, sun, tub, tug, us

Target Skills: Consonants *qu, z*
quit, zip

Words with Previously Taught Skills
big, can, digs, dog, fit, gets, has, hops, hot, in, is, it, naps, sits

High-Frequency Words

New
good, many

Previously Taught
a, help, play, the, we, with